EXTRE

CARS

DAVID JEFFERIS

W
FRANKLIN WATTS
LONDON•SYDNEY

This edition 2009

First published in 2005 by
Franklin Watts
338 Euston Road
London NW1 3BH

Franklin Watts Australia
Level 17/207 Kent Street
Sydney, NSW 2000

© 2005 Franklin Watts

EXTREME MACHINES: CARS
Created for Franklin Watts by
Q2A Creative
Editor: Chester Fisher
Designer: Mini Dhawan
Picture Researcher: Jyoti Sethi

A CIP catalogue record for this book is available from the British Library.

ISBN 978 0 7496 8953 7

Printed in China

Dewey number: 629.228

Franklin Watts is a division of Hachette Children's Books, an Hachette Livre UK company.
www.hachettelivre.co.uk

PICTURE CREDITS

Front cover: DaimlerChrysler, Back cover: vwmpress@motorpics.co.za
pp. 4 middle (National Motor Museum, Beaulieu), 5 top (National Motor Museum, Beaulieu),
6 bottom (National Motor Museum, Beaulieu), 6-7 top (National Motor Museum, Beaulieu),
8 middle (mclaren.com), 8 top (Porsche AG), 10 top (hotrodscustomstuff.com),
10 bottom (Street Rods by Michael, Bill Kyzer), 11 top (Martin Wollny motorsnippets.com),
12-13 bottom (National Motor Museum, Beaulieu), 13 top ('Joker' Hummer pictures supplied
by XoticLimos.Com), 13 middle(go-stretch.com), 14 bottom (Teemu Mottonen/teemu.net),
15 top (DaimlerChrysler), 16 top (Jim Murphy), 17 top (Santa Pod Raceway),
17 middle (Santa Pod Raceway), 18 bottom (Citroën Communication),
19 top (vwmpress@motorpics.co.za), 19 bottom (vwmpress@motorpics.co.za),
20 bottom (Christian Wannyn, Lions Club, Le Bourget, Original at the Palais de
Compiègne, France), 21 top (Jeremy Davey© SSC Programme Ltd), 22 bottom (Eric Seltzer),
23 top (Courtesy of Universal Studios Licencing Inc), 24 top (CARL SCHUPPEL),
25 top (Gibbs Aquada), 26 bottom (David Fewchuk), 27 top (BMW), 27 middle (BMW),
28 top (National Motor Museum, Beaulieu), 28 bottom (National Motor Museum, Beaulieu),
29 top (National Motor Museum, Beaulieu), 29 bottom (mclaren.com).

CONTENTS

The First Cars   4

Big and Small   6

Supercars   8

Hot Rods   10

Stretch Limos   12

Top Racers   14

Dragsters   16

Rally Racers   18

Speed on Wheels   20

Star Cars   22

Wow Wheels   24

Future Cars   26

Timeline   28

Glossary   30

Index   32

The age of the car started in 1886, with the three-wheeled 'motorwagen' of German inventor Carl Benz.

DAIMLER AND BENZ

The motorwagen was a three-wheeler, but in 1886 another German – Gottlieb Daimler – developed a car with four wheels, the layout that has been standard ever since. Both vehicles used the newly-invented petrol engine.

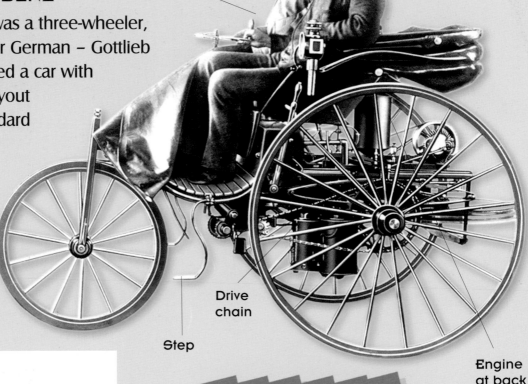

Steering tiller

Drive chain

Step

Engine at back

BENZ MOTORWAGEN 1886

TYPE	First car
SEATS	Bench seat for 2
SPEED	14 kph (9 mph)
POWER	1 petrol engine

The Benz three-wheeler had no steering wheel – instead, it had a lever called a tiller.

LONG JOURNEY

In 1888 Benz's wife, Bertha, made the first long-distance car journey, between the German towns of Mannheim and Pforzheim. The car was an improved model, but even so the trip took all day and needed several stops to repair faults.

This Renault won the first French Grand Prix race in 1906, covering a distance of 1,239 km (770 miles) in two days.

SPEED KINGS

Soon, there were many other people making cars. They all used speed to show off their new machines. The first official race was held in 1895, between Paris and Bordeaux, in France. Soon the world went race-mad, but the 1903 Paris-Madrid event was a killer – there were so many accidents that the race was stopped and the cars were all sent back to Paris by train!

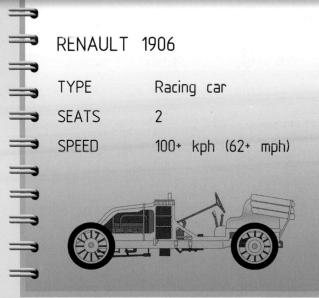

RENAULT 1906

TYPE	Racing car
SEATS	2
SPEED	100+ kph (62+ mph)

web

FINDER

http://www.mercedesbenz.com/mbcom/international/
international_website/en/com/international_home/home/
heritage/history.html#mainnav
This site gives you lots of information on the early pioneers.

BIG AND SMALL

Most cars are made in fairly standard sizes, usually about 4.3-5.5 metres (14-18 feet) long. But a few cars have been made that are very different.

TINY GERMAN

The Smart FourTwo is the shortest petrol-engined car in full production, at just over 2.5 metres (8.2 feet) long. Driving carefully, a Smart driver can expect to travel nearly 25 kilometres on a litre of fuel (70 miles per gallon) – so the car is very economical, too. The Smart is also a great car to park easily.

The Smart comes in open and closed types. There's not much room for shopping bags, but two bikes can be carried on a special rack.

Smarts come in patterns as well as plain colours

Plastic body panels

Two seats

SMART FOURTWO

TYPE	Economy micro-car
SEATS	2
SPEED	134 kph (83 mph)
POWER	One 3-cylinder petrol engine

Overall length was 6.4 m (21 ft).

The Bugatti Royale had a silver elephant mascot at the front. The eyes were a pair of red jewels.

Bonnet was more than 1.5 m (7 ft) long

BUGATTI ROYALE

The Bugatti Royale was designed in the late 1920s and probably has more 'extremes' to its name than any other car. It is the most expensive car ever – in 1931 you would have paid $32,000 for one of only six Royales ever made. As an antique, Royales are worth even more – in 1990 a Japanese company paid a staggering $15 million for a Royale!

BUGATTI ROYALE COUPE DE VILLE

TYPE	Luxury car
SEATS	5
SPEED	193 kph (120 mph)
POWER	One 8-cylinder petrol engine

web

FINDER

http://www.ktsmotorsportsgarage.com/rodeo98/ pages/bugatti.html
This enthusiast site has details and pictures of Bugattis and other great classic cars.
http://www.thesmart.co.uk/
Find out about Smart cars at the home site.

SUPERCARS

Supercars have extremely high performance and great looks – and they usually have a sky-high price tag, too!

ULTIMATE CAR?

The first McLaren F1 was sold in 1994, for a mind-boggling £635,000. But for this money, a McLaren owner got a car that was extreme in every way, and is still reckoned as the one to beat. The acceleration is shattering – the car will go from a standstill to 161 kilometres/hour (100 miles/hour) in just 6.3 seconds, and top speed is another record-breaker at 386 kilometres/hour (240 miles/hour)!

McLAREN F1

TYPE	Performance car
SEATS	3
SPEED	387 kph (240 mph), a 1998 record
POWER	1 V-12 petrol engine

Driver's central seat

Carbon-fibre and aluminium alloy

Like many supercars, the McLaren F1 has flip-up 'scissor-action' doors.

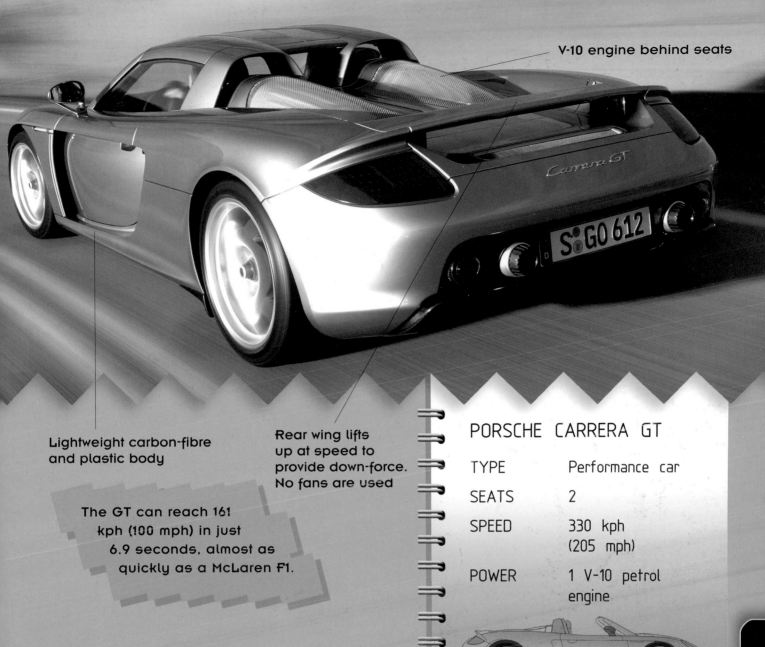

V-10 engine behind seats

Carrera GT

S•GO 612

Lightweight carbon-fibre and plastic body

Rear wing lifts up at speed to provide down-force. No fans are used

The GT can reach 161 kph (100 mph) in just 6.9 seconds, almost as quickly as a McLaren F1.

PORSCHE CARRERA GT

TYPE	Performance car
SEATS	2
SPEED	330 kph (205 mph)
POWER	1 V-10 petrol engine

GERMAN CHALLENGE

The Carrera GT is Porsche's attempt at beating the McLaren, though the figures show that it's not quite in the same class. It's slower, at 'just' 330 kilometres/hour (205 miles/hour), and has two seats. Even so, supercar drivers reckon that you get most of an F1's performance for half the price, about £323,000.

web

FINDER

http://www.mclarencars.com/content/sections/mainfr/gall.htm
The McLaren site has some great pictures and videos to download.
http://www3.uk.porsche.com/english/gbr/home.htm
Porsche's site gives you facts about all its cars, including the Carrera GT.

HOT RODS

Hot rods are often made lower at the front than the back, to give them a sportier, racier look.

Hot rods are cars that have been changed or rebuilt to make them faster and better looking.

MIX AND MATCH

Hot rods are often built using parts from a number of different cars. The body of a 1930s Ford Coupe might be fitted with brakes from a second car, steering from a third car, and seats from a fourth. Some parts might have to be specially made for the car.

1930s COUPE HOT ROD

1930s ENGINE	3.6 litres Ford
HOT ROD ENGINE	4.4 to 5.8 litres Ford or Chevrolet

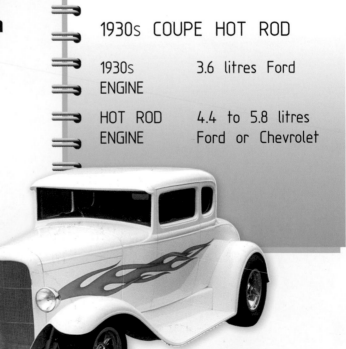

The Pierson Coupe is one of the fastest hot rods ever built.

PIERSON FORD COUPE

ORIGINAL CAR	1934 Ford Coupe
ENGINE	4.4 l
1934 TOP SPEED	125 kph (78 mph)
HOT ROD TOP SPEED	365 kph (227 mph)

RECORD BREAKER

One famous hot rod is called the Pierson Coupe (say *koo-pay*). A coupe is a two-door car with a sloping back. The Pierson Coupe started as an ordinary Ford car made in 1934. It was rebuilt as a super-fast hot rod. It was so fast that it set a number of speed records.

web

FINDER

http://www.bryantauto.com/Pierson%20Coupe%20Story.html
Read about the history of the Pierson Coupe hot rod.
http://hotrod.com/featuredvehicles/6042
See more pictures of hot rods and how they are made.

Hot-rod owners often take part in rallies. Every car is polished until it gleams!

STRETCH LIMOS

Limousines, or limos, are luxury cars. Stretch limos are limousines that have been made longer.

CUTTING CARS IN TWO

To make a stretch limo, a brand new and very expensive luxury car is cut in two. The cut is made just behind the front seats. Then an extra length of car body is built in the middle to make the whole car longer.

PUTTING ON WEIGHT

When a car is stretched, it becomes heavier. It may even double in weight. Some of its parts have to be replaced because of this extra weight. A car is held up by springs, so stretch limos need stronger springs to support their greater weight. A heavier car is harder to stop, so stretch limos also need more powerful brakes.

LINCOLN TOWN CAR STRETCH LIMO

ENGINE	4.6 l	STRETCH LENGTH	8.5 m (28 ft)
UNSTRETCHED LENGTH	5.5 m (18 ft)	POWER	239 hp

The Lincoln Town Car is a popular choice for building stretch limos.

This Hummer has been stretched to twice its normal size.

CARS FOR STRETCHING

Luxury Cadillac, Lincoln and Chrysler cars are the most popular for building stretch limos, but any car can be used. One of the smallest cars in the world, the Mini, has been stretched. There are even stretched versions of military vehicles called Hummers!

HUMMER H2 STRETCH LIMO

DOORS	5
CAPACITY	20-24 people
ENGINE	Vortex 8
UNSTRETCHED LENGTH	4.5 m (15 ft)
STRETCHED LENGTH	9 m (30 ft)

A view inside a 'stretch' (left).

web

FINDER

http://www.lcwlimo.com/buildprocess.htm
See how a stretch limo is built.
http://www.dabryancoach.com/docs/model_detail/120_lincoln.html
See how luxurious a stretch limo is.

TOP RACERS

Each year races take place to decide who is the champion driver and car manufacturer. Formula One and NASCAR races are the ultimate tests of car design and driver skills.

PRANCING HORSE

The most famous name in Formula One (F1) is Ferrari, from Italy. The firm started in the 1940s and has raced every season since F1 started in 1950. You can spot a Ferrari easily, for the cars are always bright red (Italy's traditional racing colour) and have Ferrari's 'prancing horse' logo on them. Their most famous driver is Michael Schumacher, who has been the World Champion seven times.

FERRARI F2004

TYPE	F1 racing car
SEATS	1
SPEED	306+ kph (190+ mph)
POWER	1 V-10 petrol engine

All F1 cars have a similar look with wide wheels and a powerful engine behind the driver.

Front and rear aerofoils force the car down onto the track

Cockpit has seat made to fit each driver

Wide tyres come in 'dry' and 'wet' versions, to suit the weather during a race

A Dodge Intrepid R/T in the NASCAR Winston Cup at the Las Vegas Motor Speedway.

RACING TO WIN

Stock-car racing, known as NASCAR, is one of the most popular motor sports in the USA. It began with normal cars being raced around oval-shaped tracks. Today, the cars are specially built for NASCAR races by major manufacturers such as Ford, Chevrolet, Dodge and Pontiac. There is fierce competition among the teams and drivers at the many races, such as the Daytona 500, to become overall champions for the year. NASCAR races draw huge crowds of over 100,000 per race.

DODGE INTREPID R/T

TYPE	Road and track car
POWER	5.7-l V8 petrol engine
SPEED	295 kph (184 mph)
DRIVE	Rear wheel

web

FINDER

http://www.thescuderia.net/
This enthusiast site has heaps of stuff about Ferraris
Also check this: *http://www.ferrari.com*

DRAGSTERS

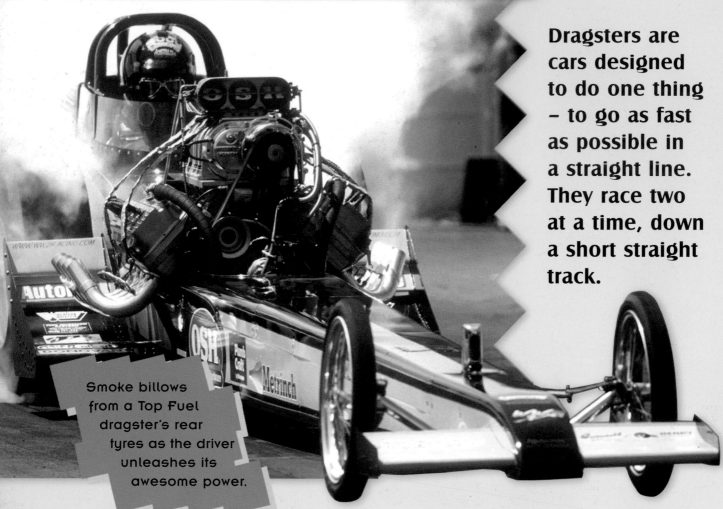

Dragsters are cars designed to do one thing – to go as fast as possible in a straight line. They race two at a time, down a short straight track.

Smoke billows from a Top Fuel dragster's rear tyres as the driver unleashes its awesome power.

AT TOP SPEED!

The fastest dragsters are called Top Fuel dragsters. They burn a fuel called nitromethane in a huge engine at the back of the car. The driver sits in front of this mighty, deafening engine. Top Fuel dragsters reach their top speed in less than five seconds, the time it takes for a whole race from start to finish! At the end of a race, they are going so fast that they have to pop out parachutes to help slow them down.

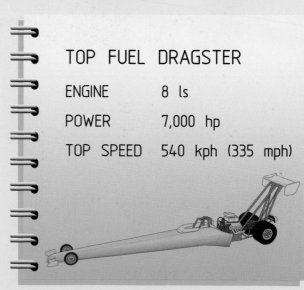

TOP FUEL DRAGSTER

ENGINE	8 ls
POWER	7,000 hp
TOP SPEED	540 kph (335 mph)

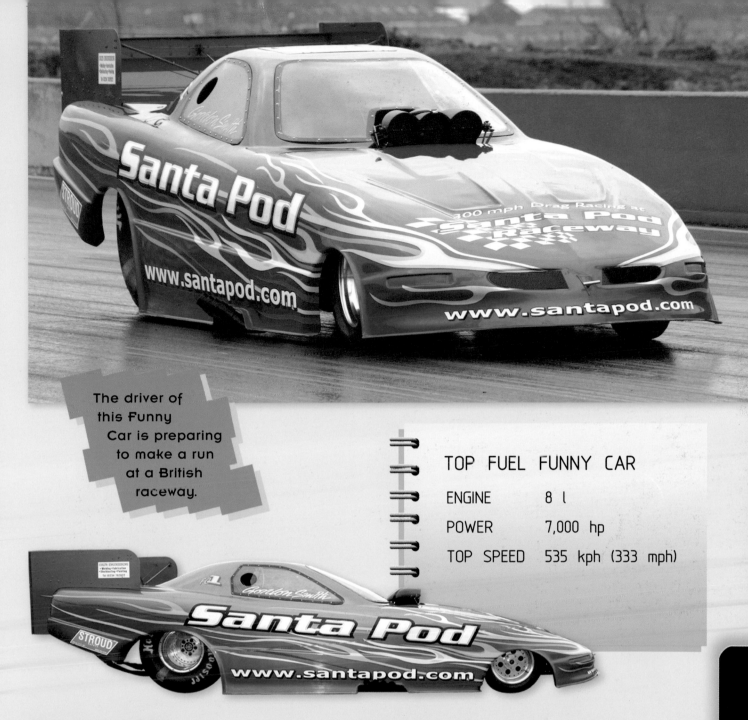

The driver of this Funny Car is preparing to make a run at a British raceway.

TOP FUEL FUNNY CAR

ENGINE	8 l
POWER	7,000 hp
TOP SPEED	535 kph (333 mph)

FUNNY CARS

Another type of dragster is the Funny Car, which is covered with a body that looks a bit like an ordinary car. Underneath its body, the engine is the same as a Top Fuel dragster engine. But the Funny Car's engine is in front of the driver. Most Funny Cars are powered by supercharged alcohol engines.

web

FINDER

http://www.nhra.com/streetlegal/whatisadragrace.html
Find out more about dragsters and drag racing in the United States.
http://www.nhra.com/streetlegal/funfacts. html<http://www.nhra.com/streetlegal/funfacts.html>
Read some amazing facts about dragsters and drag racing.

RALLY RACERS

Rallies are long-distance events taking place on roads, dirt tracks, snow, or ice. The cars are based on the ones on sale to the public, but they have been adapted for extreme conditions.

WORLD RALLY CHAMPIONSHIP

The World Rally Championship (WRC) takes teams around the world each year in a series of events that last from January to November. But rallying itself has a long history – the first one was held in 1907, from China to France. The winner took two months to drive 12,000 kilometres (7,500 miles) between Peking and Paris.

KEEPING ON COURSE

To win a rally today, it's essential to have a four-wheel drive (4WD) car in which all the wheels are driven by the engine. With 4WD, cars can scramble around corners quicker and drive through mud or sand more easily.

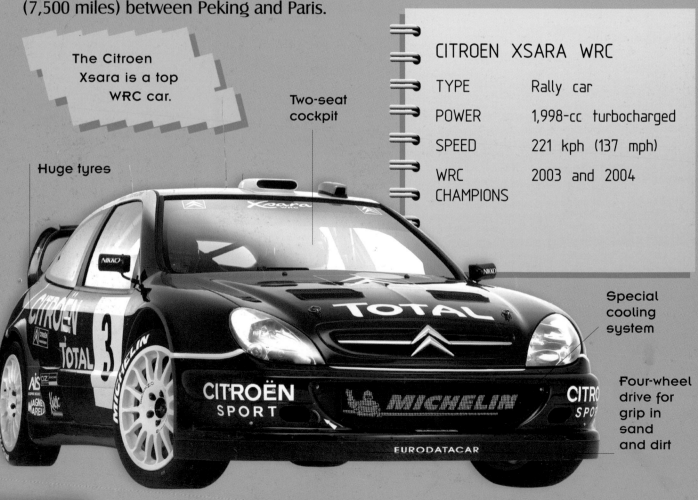

The Citroen Xsara is a top WRC car.

Two-seat cockpit

Huge tyres

Special cooling system

Four-wheel drive for grip in sand and dirt

CITROEN XSARA WRC

TYPE	Rally car
POWER	1,998-cc turbocharged
SPEED	221 kph (137 mph)
WRC CHAMPIONS	2003 and 2004

The Rally Touarag is about as different from the standard car as possible. The standard Touarag is a comfy 4WD car.

DEADLY DAKAR

The most extreme rally of all is the Paris-Dakar, which finishes up at Dakar in Senegal. In 2005 it followed a winding route through France, Spain and four African countries. Special timed stages were held along the way. The Dakar is a dangerous race – accidents are common and racers sometimes get killed.

VOLKSWAGEN TOUARAG DAKAR

TYPE	Dakar Rally car
SEATS	2 (standard car seats 5 people)
SPEED	209+ kph (130+ mph)
POWER	15-cylinder diesel engine

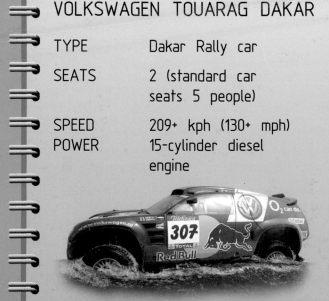

web

FINDER

http://www.wrc.com
The WRC site tells you almost all you need to know about rally cars.
http://www.volkswagen.co.nz/concepts/conceptT/downloads.asp
This Volkswagen site has details of the Touarag Dakar and other interesting cars.

SPEED ON WHEELS

Car drivers have been trying to smash speed records since the earliest days of the automobile. The cars here were built almost a century apart, yet the aim was the same for both – to be fastest in the world.

RED DEVIL

One of the first speed-record drivers was Camille Jenatzy, a Belgian nicknamed 'Red Devil' for his extremely long, red beard. In 1898 he put the finishing touches to a bullet-shaped car, powered by sets of electric batteries.

NEVER SATISFIED

On 1 May 1899, Jenatzy's electric car, La Jamais Contente ('The Never Satisfied'), became the fastest car in the world when Jenatzy drove it along a track near Paris. His speed may not sound much today, at just 106 kilometres/hour (66 miles/hour), but it was fast enough to hold the record for three years!

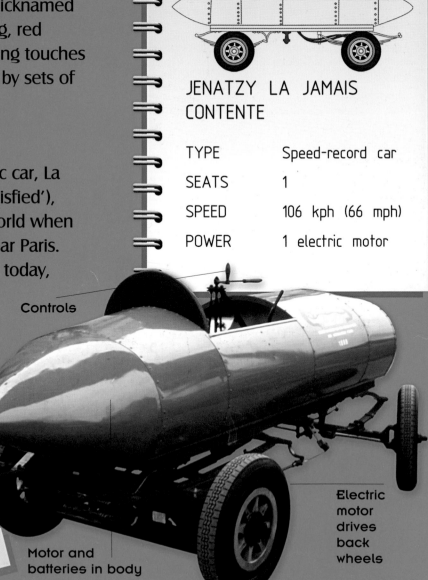

JENATZY LA JAMAIS CONTENTE

TYPE	Speed-record car
SEATS	1
SPEED	106 kph (66 mph)
POWER	1 electric motor

Controls

Metal bodywork

La Jamais Contente was the first car to go faster than 100 kph (62 mph).

Motor and batteries in body

Electric motor drives back wheels

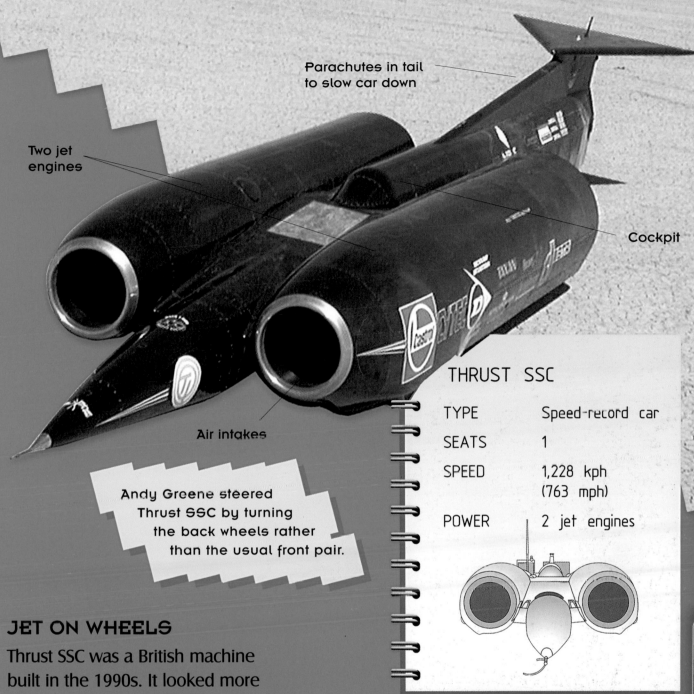

Parachutes in tail
to slow car down

Two jet
engines

Cockpit

Air intakes

Andy Greene steered
Thrust SSC by turning
the back wheels rather
than the usual front pair.

THRUST SSC

TYPE	Speed-record car
SEATS	1
SPEED	1,228 kph (763 mph)
POWER	2 jet engines

JET ON WHEELS

Thrust SSC was a British machine built in the 1990s. It looked more like a fighter plane than a car, with sleek tail-fin and two jet engines, one each side of the needle-nosed body. And driver Andy Greene was a jet fighter pilot. In 1997, Thrust SSC smashed all records, travelling at almost 1,228 kilometres/hour (763 miles/hour), hurtling across the flat lands of the Black Rock desert, in the USA.

FINDER

http://www.speedace.info/jamais.htm
This site gives you lots of information on speed records, including Jenatzy's car.
http://www.thrustssc.com/
This is the home site of Thrust SSC, with many details of the car.

STAR CARS

Many extreme cars have been made for TV series and Hollywood films. Most of them are based on real cars, though you can hardly tell after the special-effects experts have done their job.

THE BATMOBILE

This was the car in which comic-hero Batman chased criminals, first on TV and then in several films. The original TV Batmobile was first shown in 1966. It was converted from a special 'concept car', the $250,000 Lincoln Futura of 11 years earlier. This had been built to show what a car of the future might look like.

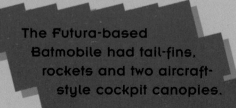

The Futura-based Batmobile had tail-fins, rockets and two aircraft-style cockpit canopies.

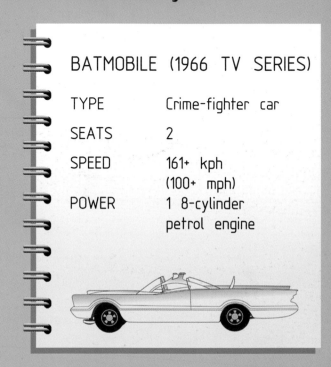

BATMOBILE (1966 TV SERIES)

TYPE	Crime-fighter car
SEATS	2
SPEED	161+ kph (100+ mph)
POWER	1 8-cylinder petrol engine

Lights

Clear canopies

Long tail-fins were popular in the 1950s

Gull-wing doors

Extra 'time travel' equipment

Only 8,583 DeLoreans were ever made. Amazingly, about 6,000 still survive today. Shown here is the version used in 'Back to the Future'.

DMC DELOREAN (MOVIE VERSION)

TYPE	Sports car
SEATS	2
SPEED	142 kph (88 mph)
POWER	1 8-cylinder petrol engine + atomic power

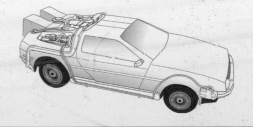

DELOREAN

The three-film series *Back to the Future* featured the DeLorean car, which was built in 1981-83. In the film the car could travel in time, provided it hit exactly 142 kilometres/hour (88 miles/hour)! The good-looking original had lift-up 'gull wing' doors that made it look quite futuristic – so all the special-effects team had to do was add some technical-looking bits and pieces to make it appear very special indeed.

web

FINDER

http://www.delorean.com/
This classic car site has details of the DeLorean and its history, and there are some for sale.
http://www.bttfmovie.com/
Find out about the three *Back to the Future* films at this site.

WOW WHEELS

Here are some of the most inventive cars ever made, vehicles that test design extremes even on water and in the air!

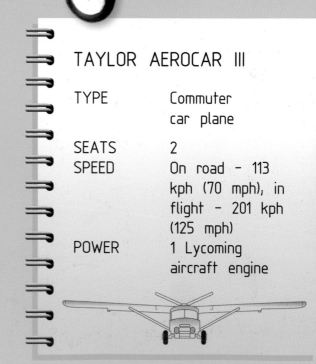

Engine compartment

Propeller

Two seats at front

The Taylor Aerocar had a 'pusher' propeller mounted at the back.

CAR WITH WINGS

The Aerocar was the brainchild of US inventor Moulton Taylor, who designed a small car to which wings and tail could be added when the owner wanted to go flying. Taylor's Aerocar III went on sale in 1956, but was ahead of its time – just six were built. Today there are plans for a brand-new version, based on a Lotus Elize sports car.

PROPELLER POWER

The earlier French Leyat Aerocar also had propeller power, though it had no wings. The 1923 design could reach 161 kilometres/hour (100 miles/hour) on a straight road, but only one was ever made.

TAYLOR AEROCAR III

TYPE	Commuter car plane
SEATS	2
SPEED	On road – 113 kph (70 mph); in flight – 201 kph (125 mph)
POWER	1 Lycoming aircraft engine

Water-jet power at the back

Fold-up wheels

SEA SPEEDER

On land the Gibbs Aquada looks and drives like any two-seater sports car. In water, the wheels fold away and the Aquada turns into a fast speedboat. The engine squirts out a rocket-like jet of water out the back, thrusting the Aquada forward at high speed. It is the world's first high-speed amphibious vehicle. The Aquada is not on sale at the moment, but could be available around 2007. About 4,000 German Amphibicars were made in the 1960s, but were much slower.

The three-seat Aquada is powerful enough to tow a water-skier.

web

FINDER

http://www.aerocar.com/
Get up-to-date with Aerocar developments here
*http://www.aquada.co.uk/aquada/homepage.jsp?
flash=true*
Here is the Aquada's home site

GIBBS AQUADA

TYPE	High-speed, amphibian sports car-boat
SEATS	3
SPEED	On land – 161 kph (100 mph); on water – 56 kph (35 mph)
POWER	1 6-cylinder petrol engine, which also powers the water-jet

EXTREME MACHINES Cars

FUTURE CARS

Researchers work hard to make cars better. A key aim is to make cars with ultra-clean engines producing little or no pollution.

SUN POWER

Solar cars are the cleanest vehicles of all, using solar-cell panels that change the energy in sunlight to electricity, which powers electric motors to turn the wheels. To test out new ideas, solar races are held in various countries. The Australian Aurora team set several records in 2005, including the first solar car to run for 24 hours – the car stopped only to change drivers, to repair a flat tyre, and to fix the radio. To break the record, Aurora's solar cells charged batteries that kept the car going at night.

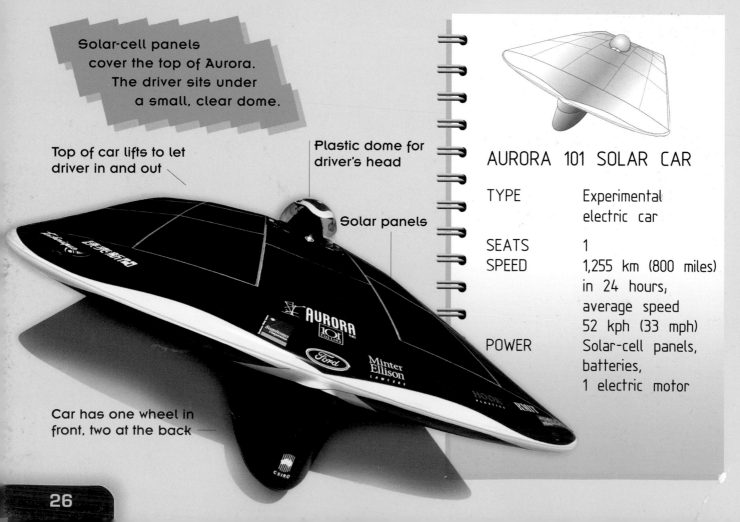

Solar-cell panels cover the top of Aurora. The driver sits under a small, clear dome.

Top of car lifts to let driver in and out

Plastic dome for driver's head

Solar panels

Car has one wheel in front, two at the back

AURORA 101 SOLAR CAR

TYPE	Experimental electric car
SEATS	1
SPEED	1,255 km (800 miles) in 24 hours; average speed 52 kph (33 mph)
POWER	Solar-cell panels, batteries, 1 electric motor

Single-seat cockpit

Lightweight bodywork

Air Intake for engine cooling

The H2R engine is based on a standard BMW unit, converted to burn hydrogen fuel.

GAS POWER

In Germany, the BMW company is working on an engine that can burn either standard petrol or hydrogen, a gas which burns so cleanly that its waste is almost entirely plain water. To test the engine, BMW built the H2R and in 2005 smashed nine world records for hydrogen cars.

BMW H2R

TYPE	Experimental hydrogen car
SEATS	1
SPEED	300 kph (186 mph)
POWER	1 hydrogen-fuelled engine

web

FINDER

http://www.aurorasolarcar.com/
This site shows information on solar power and the Aurora 101 car.
http://www.bmwtransact.com/hydrogen/ cars_h2r.htm
Visit this site to check out BMW's hydrogen-fuel research.

TIMELINE

1886

First successful petrol-engine cars developed by Carl Benz (a three-wheel design) and Gottlieb Daimler (four-wheel design), in Germany.

1888

Bertha Benz becomes the first woman driver and makes the first long-distance journey by car, taking her two sons, Eugen and Richard, on the 100-km (61-mi) trip.

1895

First big car race held, from Paris to Bordeaux and back. It was won by Emile Lavassor, driving a Panhard. He averaged 24 kph (15 mph) over the 1,178-km (732-mi) course. This was an amazing feat – at the time, cars were unreliable and most roads were no better than dusty or muddy trails.

1896

First race on a closed circuit held in Rhode Island, USA. Cars raced for five laps around a 1.6-km (1-mi) dirt-and-cinder track in a park – an electric car was the winner.

1903

First big racing accidents during the Paris-to-Madrid race, which stopped before the drivers had even left France. The only female driver was a Madame du Gast, who became a heroine for stopping to look after the injured.

1905

Tourist Trophy race held on Isle of Man. It is still held every year and is the oldest race still running.

1907

First long-distance rally held, from China to Britain. The rally was repeated in 1990, but this time the direction was reversed, from London to Beijing!

1908

Ford Model T 'Tin Lizzie' goes on sale. From the start, the car was a success and by 1922 one million were being made every year.

1927

The Ford Model T is replaced by the improved Ford Model A.

1937

Design completed for the Volkswagen (VW) Beetle, as a cheap-to-buy 'people's car'. The Beetle holds the record for biggest production of the same design, at more than 21 million when VW stopped making it in 2003.

1958

Ford Edsel launched in the United States and reckoned to be the biggest failure ever, as Ford lost about $300 million on the car. Today an Edsel is a highly-prized classic car!

1959

Bruce McLaren from New Zealand becomes the youngest-ever Grand Prix (GP) winner, after taking the lead in the US Grand Prix in Florida. The oldest-ever GP winner was Tazio Nuvolari, an Italian driver who won the French Grand Prix in 1946, when he was 53 years old.

1969

Closest-ever Le Mans win, when drivers in a Ford GT40 and Porsche 908 diced for victory. After 24 hours flat-out racing, the GT40 won by just 100 m (328 ft)!

1977

Longest-ever rally held, from London to Sydney. Distance covered was 31,107 km (19,329 mi). Today's rallies are usually shorter, but the World Rally Championship (WRC) is a hard-fought set of rallies during a year. It's considered to be at least as tough as any longer, single rally held in the past.

1992

McLaren F1 launched as the most powerful production car ever made. Six years later the car was still setting records – in 1998 it reached 386.7 kph (240.1 mph) at a Volkswagen test track in Germany.

1999

White Lightning Electric Streamliner is driven at 395.821 kph (245.523 mph) to become the world's fastest electric vehicle. White Lightning was driven by Patrick Rummerfield at Bonneville Salt Flats, U.S., on October 22.

2004

Enzo is Ferrari's most expensive performance car for sale. Without extras, the cost is £418,198! The Mercedes SLR McLaren is a close competitor if you have the money – painted only black or silver, the car can go from a standstill to 100 kph (62 mph) in just 3.8 seconds, and costs about £315,000!

2005

Aurora solar-electric car record is taken for going continuously for 24 hours, even at night, when the car continues using batteries that were charged during daylight hours.

GLOSSARY

AEROFOIL

A wing-like fin on a performance car that helps to keep it firmly on the road or track by using the push of passing air to create a downward pressure, called down-force.

ALUMINIUM

A light but strong metal used for construction.

AMPHIBIOUS CAR

A car that can travel on water as well as land.

CARBON-FIBRE

A plastic material with fibres of carbon added during manufacture. It is very light and very strong, so is used a lot for racing cars.

CIRCUIT

A track used for racing that is not open for other vehicles. A few circuits, such as Le Mans, have some parts of the circuit that are public roads, but these are closed to traffic on race days.

COCKPIT

Part of the car where the crew sit – may have one or two seats, depending on the car.

CONCEPT CAR

A one-of-a-kind futuristic, experimental car usually appearing at motor shows to stimulate interest in the manufacturer's products. Concept cars push car design forward, but only a few reach the production stage.

CUSTOM CAR

A standard model of car that has been adapted by its owner to make it look or drive the way he or she wants it.

DIESEL ENGINE

A type of internal-combustion engine that burns thick diesel instead of petrol (see petrol engine).

DRAG RACER

A car that has been specially designed to take in short, high-speed acceleration races.

FORMULA

Set of rules that apply to a particular kind of racing. The formula controls how a car is made, the size of its engine, its weight and many other details.

FOUR-WHEEL DRIVE (4WD)

A system that transfers engine power to all four wheels. 4WD provides superior traction compared with front- or rear-wheel drive.

GRAND PRIX

French words for 'big race', and mostly used when talking about Formula One.

HORSEPOWER (HP)

The unit for measuring the power output of an engine. Higher horsepower increases the vehicle's top speed. One horsepower is defined as lifting 33,000 pounds one foot per minute. The term was first used by the inventor James Watt when he wanted to compare the power of a steam engine to that of the horse it replaced.

HOT ROD

Any car that has been rebuilt or modified to increase its speed and acceleration.

HYDROGEN

Flammable gas used in some experimental engines, such as the BMW H2R.

INTERNAL-COMBUSTION ENGINE

Any engine in which the fuel is consumed in the interior of the engine rather than outside of the engine.

NASCAR

National Association for Stock Car Auto Racing. The organisation that promotes and regulates stock-car racing in the USA.

PETROL

A liquid made from oil that burns easily and is the main fuel for internal-combustion engines.

PETROL ENGINE

Type of engine that uses petroleum liquid as its fuel. The engine itself is called an internal-combustion (ic) engine, because it burns fuel in cylinders inside the engine. The cylinders can vary in number and arrangement, from simple ones such as 4 in-line to complex designs such as V-12.

POLLUTION

Chemical waste in the unburnt parts of a car exhaust. Today's engines produce much less pollution than earlier types, and future engines should make even less.

SOLAR CELL

Silicon material that changes the energy in sunlight to electricity. Solar cells are usually made in the form of thin, flat panels that can be laid out to catch the Sun's rays.

SPONSOR

A company that pays a racing team for advertising its products on the cars.

STAGE

A specially timed section of a rally. On stages, cars normally leave at one-minute intervals, with crews aiming to finish at an exact time. They lose points if they are late and often, if they are early too.

Note to parents and teachers:
Every effort has been made by the Publishers to ensure that the websites in this book are suitable for children, that they are of the highest educational value, and that they contain no inappropriate or offensive material. However, because of the nature of the Internet, it is impossible to guarantee that the contents of these sites will not be altered. We strongly advise that Internet access is supervised by a responsible adult.

INDEX

A

Aurora 101 26, 27, 29

B

Back to the Future 23
Batmobile 22
Benz, C 4, 28
Benz Motorwagen 4
BMW H2R 27, 31
Bugatti Royale 7

C

Championship, World
  Rally 18, 19, 29
Citroen Xsara 18
cars
  amphibious 25, 30
  classic 7, 23
  concept 22, 30
  dragster see dragster
  experimental 26, 27,
  30
  fastest 20, 21
  flying 24
  funny 7
  history of 4, 5, 28, 29
  hydrogen 27, 31
  luxury 7, 12, 13
  racing 5, 14-17, 28, 30
  rally 18, 19
  solar 26, 29, 31
  sports 23, 25

D

Daimler, G 4, 28
Daytona 500 15
DMC DeLorean 23
Dodge Intrepid RIT 15
dragster 16, 17, 30

F

Ferrari F2004 14, 15, 29
Ford 15
  Coupe 10, 11
  Edsel 29
  Model T 28
  Pierson Coupe 11
Formula One 14, 30

G

Gibbs Aquada 25
Grand Prix 5, 29, 30

H

hot rod 10, 11, 31
Hummer H2 13

L

La Jamais Contente 20
Leyat Aerocar 24
limousine 12, 13
Lincoln
  Futura 22
  Town Car 12

M

McLaren F1 8, 9, 29

N

NASCAR (National
  Association for Stock
  Car Auto Racing) 14,
  15, 31

P

pollution 26, 27, 31
Porsche Carrera GT 9

R

racing 28, 29, 30
  drag 16, 17, 30
  stock-car 15, 31
rally 11, 18, 19, 28, 29
Renault 5

S

Smart FourTwo 6, 7
supercar 8, 9

T

Taylor Aerocar III 24, 25
Thrust SSC 21

V

Volkswagen Touarag
  Dakar 19

32